Say NO and Go

Stranger Safety

How to Be Safe!

by Jill Urban Donahue   illustrated by Bob Masheris

Trusted Adults:

Grandma
Grandpa
Uncle Sal
Mrs. Jensen
Pastor Paul

PICTURE WINDOW BOOKS
Minneapolis, Minnesota

Special thanks to our advisers for their expertise:
Sandi Schnorenberg, Associate Deputy Director
Mankato (Minnesota) Public Safety

Terry Flaherty, Ph.D., Professor of English
Minnesota State University, Mankato

Editor: Jill Kalz
Designer: Abbey Fitzgerald
Page Production: Melissa Kes
Art Director: Nathan Gassman
Associate Managing Editor: Christianne Jones
The illustrations in this book were created digitally.

Picture Window Books
151 Good Counsel Drive
P.O. Box 669
Mankato, MN 56002-0669
877-845-8392
www.picturewindowbooks.com

Printed in the United States of America.

 All books published by Picture Window Books
are manufactured with paper containing at least
10 percent post-consumer waste.

Library of Congress Cataloging-in-Publication Data
Donahue, Jill Urban.
Say no and go : stranger safety / by Jill Urban Donahue ;
illustrated by Bob Masheris.
p. cm. — (How to be safe!)
Includes index.
ISBN-13: 978-1-4048-4826-9 (library binding)
1. Safety education—Juvenile literature. 2. Children
and strangers—Juvenile literature. 3. Children—
Crimes against—Prevention—Juvenile literature.
I. Masheris, Robert. II. Title.
HQ770.7.D67 2009
613.6083—dc22   2008006423

A stranger is anyone you don't know. Most people are good and kind. But some people aren't. You can't tell for sure just by looking at someone. If you follow a few simple rules about strangers, you'll stay safe!

Rani's mom and dad are packed and ready to go. They are going to the hospital to have a baby.

The doorbell rings. Rani lets her dad answer the door.

Safety Tip

Never open the door by yourself, even if you think you know who it is. Let an adult answer the door.

Grandma stays with Rani. She is on the trusted adults list Rani's parents made. It is OK for Rani to stay with trusted adults. It is OK to ride in their cars and to accept things from them.

Trusted Adults:

Grandma
Grandpa
Uncle Sal
Mrs. Jensen
Pastor Paul

Safety Tip

Ask your parents to give you a list of five trusted adults. Study the list so you know who is on it.

Some people are not strangers, but they're not on Rani's list, either. These are people Rani "kind of" knows. If they want to give Rani a treat or take her someplace, she must ask her parents first.

Safety Tip

People you "kind of" know may be any people that you have seen before but don't know well. Examples may include the mail carrier, neighbors down the block, or people at your place of worship.

Grandma talks to Rani about stranger safety. She quizzes Rani about her address. Then Grandma quizzes her about her telephone number.

Safety Tip

If a stranger comes to your door and will not leave, do not open the door. Call 9-1-1. That's the number for emergencies. It's helpful to know your address and phone number. Stay on the phone until the 9-1-1 person tells you to hang up.

Rani doesn't give her address or phone number to strangers on the Internet. She doesn't give her information to strangers on the phone or in person, either.

The phone rings. Rani lets Grandma answer it. Rani's dad has good news. Rani has a new baby brother!

Safety Tip

Talk to your parents about when it's OK to answer the phone and when it's not.

EXTENSION

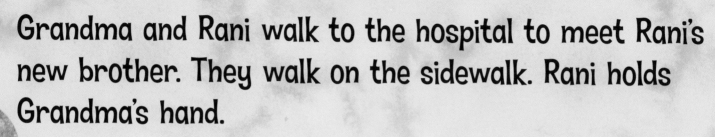

Grandma and Rani walk to the hospital to meet Rani's new brother. They walk on the sidewalk. Rani holds Grandma's hand.

16

Safety Tip

When you go outside your home, go with a friend. Make sure your parents know where you are.

A strange car pulls up by Grandma and Rani. Rani has never seen the car before. She stays on the sidewalk with Grandma.

Safety Tip

If a stranger tries to get you to leave with him or her, yell "No!" as loud as you can and run away. Remember: Say no and go.

Rani knows the man in the car. It's Uncle Sal! Rani and Grandma get in. They make a stop at a store to buy a baby gift. Rani stays near Grandma in the store.

Safety Tip

If you ever get lost in a store, ask someone who works there to help you. Then stay with that person until your family member finds you. Never leave the store or go out to the car by yourself.

At the hospital, Rani holds her little brother. She is going to be a good big sister. Now that she knows about stranger safety, she will teach her new brother, Simon, how to be safe, too!

To Learn More

More Books to Read

Llewellyn, Claire. *Around Town*. Hauppauge, N.Y.: Barron's Educational Series, 2006.

Pancella, Peggy. *Stranger Danger*. Chicago: Heinemann Library, 2004.

Raatma, Lucia. *Safety Around Strangers*. Chanhassen, Minn.: Child's World, 2005.

Raatma, Lucia. *Safety in Public Places*. Chanhassen, Minn.: Child's World, 2005.

On the Web

FactHound offers a safe, fun way to find Web sites related to topics in this book. All of the sites on FactHound have been researched by our staff.

1. Visit *www.facthound.com*
2. Type in this special code: 1404848266
3. Click on the FETCH IT button.

Your trusty FactHound will fetch the best sites for you!

Index

Look for all of the books in the How to Be Safe! series:

Contain the Flame: Outdoor Fire Safety

Play It Safe: Playground Safety

Ride Right: Bicycle Safety

Say No and Go: Stranger Safety